Over 300 top tips and

Paul Smith

TOP TIPS

FOR CLIMBING COACHES

First published 2009

Published in Great Britain 2009 by Pesda Press
Unit 22, Galeri, Doc Victoria
Caernarfon, Gwynedd
LL55 1SQ

ISBN: 978-1-906095-20-8

Printed and bound in Poland. www.hussarbooks.pl

Acknowledgements

I must thank the following people for their contributions, support and advice:

Adam Harmer, Alan Halewood, Jon 'Spike' Green, Giles Stone, Dr Rebecca Ward, James Thacker, Mark Stevenson, Mike Swan, Guy Jarvis, Alex Jeffrey, Mark Beecher, Claudia Sarner, Mark Busby at Big Stone and of course, Franco Ferrero and Pete Wood at Pesda Press.

Special thanks need to go to FiveTen and Pyranha for their continued support.

About the Author

Paul Smith has taught climbing all across the UK and worldwide. He holds the Mountain Instructor Award and is an Aspirant Level 5 Kayak Coach. As well as being a full member of the Association of Mountaineering Instructors, he is also an Institute for Outdoor Learning Accredited Practitioner. Paul divides his time between working as the Head of Outdoor Learning at a state school in Worcestershire and running his own business Rock and Water Adventures, which offers technical advice for outdoor centres and climbing walls. Paul is a Climbing Wall Award (CWA) and Single Pitch Award (SPA) provider for Mountain Leader Training England (MLTE).

Introduction

Wherever you are on the long ladder of teaching other people to climb, as an informal coach to friends at the local crag, or working through the National Governing Body awards from the Climbing Wall Award (CWA) to the Mountain Instructor Certificate (MIC), people always have tips to offer. This book puts together, in one place, a wide selection of tips for you to try out.

You will probably already have come across the analogy of the coach's toolbox; a collection of their favourite 'tools' to aid coaching. These may be aids to observation, exercises, games, similes, analogies and so on. An experienced coach will have a different tool for almost every situation. Some will be well-worn favourites and some will lurk at the bottom of the toolbox, almost forgotten.

A coach's brain is their toolbox; some have their tools in neat compartments while others will rummage around till they find the right one for the job. Everyone will organise their toolbox in their own way.

To that end no attempt has been made to organise this collection of tools in a logical order. Browse through them, select the ones you think you might find useful, experiment with them, customise them to suit your needs and style and then they will have found their place in your toolbox.

TOP TIPS

1. If your group is bored, you are boring.

2. Your personal safety is important don't take short cuts!

3. Use a suitable and adaptable approach to rigging – don't rely on that one system that was described to you or shown in a book.

4_ Read the manufacturer's instructions when buying new equipment and be sure that you really understand them.

5_ Use equipment as advised by the manufacturer.

6_ When using a direct belay on a single pitch climb, think high anchors and small ledges in order to reduce any environmental damage or damage to your ropes.

7_ Always make sure that you explain not only how, but also why you do things. Understanding the reasons for doing something makes everything so much easier to remember.

8_ Keep things simple, safe and slick.

9_ Remember that the group is made up of individuals.

10_ Don't get lazy and rely on handouts – many people respond best to verbal communication.

11_ Never judge people by their appearance.

12_ Carry a roll of rubbish sacks.

13_ Go to a local carpet shop and buy a few carpet tiles

for the top of the crags to stop rope wear.

14_ Have your climber descend from just outside of

arm's reach the first time or face the consequences

when they refuse to let go 15m up.

15_ Don't be upset that not everyone wants to be
a climber – give them credit for trying.

16_ If you have to encourage and cajole someone every inch
of the way up you may have an even harder time getting
them down again. Let them climb to the height they are
happy with and then come back and try again later.

17_ If you have to encourage and cajole someone every inch of the way up, you may have chosen the wrong route.

18_ Knowing what your clients want from their climbing session should inform how you run that session.

19_ Give the clients what they need, not just what they want.

20_ Ask your clients what they want out of the day.

21_ Never work beyond your ability,

experience or insurance cover.

22_ If you can no longer do something, be

honest with yourself and your clients.

23. Some kids are fat, some kids are thin – cater to everyone.

24. Be knowledgeable of what is around you and
   don't bluff, as one day you will get caught out.

25. Insurance – its better to have it and not need
   it, than to need it and not have it.

26_   Experience counts – lack of experience shows.

27_   When climbing multi-pitch routes with novice climbers try
       to choose a relatively straight route without big traverses,
       with good line of sight and an easy lower-off or escape.

28. In some situations, a guide-plate belay device (like

    the Petzl Reverso) and big cordelettes, or slings,

    can make your life much easier on the belays.

29. When assessing SPAs, move away from students while

    they are working; don't hover and make them nervous.

30_ Learn about the local flora, geology and history. Your days out will be richer and so will those of your clients.

31_ Have your own epics and adventures – don't confine your climbing to work.

32_ You never know it all – be humble and keep on learning.

33_   Don't be afraid to let someone know if you
       have learnt something from them.

34_   Gaffer tape is excellent; have some in your
       rucksack wrapped around your water bottle.

35_   Just because someone doesn't climb hard routes
       doesn't mean that they will not be a great instructor.

36. A mobile phone, first aid kit and group shelter
     are all essential items of equipment that you
     should have with you when working.

37. The easiest way for you to deal with problems on a
     single pitch crag is to lower them to the floor.

38. Be able to lower them to the floor.

39. Think about the simplest method for doing a complex task and try that first.

40. Harnesses are worn over the top of all layers of clothing; that way they are easier to check.

41_ When teaching tying in, always go from the top down when threading the rope through a harness, to avoid tying only into their leg loops!

42_ A big overhand knot on the bight on the dead end of the rope is a quick and efficient way of securing people while on a big comfortable ledge.

43_ On a multi-pitch stance, to avoid tangling ropes, try to have the person that will be leaving the belay first clipped in front of the rest and on the side that they will be leaving from. Clip the rest of the climbers in the order that they will be leaving.

44. A stacked abseil has it's place (on a multi-pitch abseil descent with experienced clients). Other methods of safeguarding the descent are usually more appropriate.

45. Protect yourself. If you are not attached to something you are not setting a good example to your group.

46_ Don't overload clients with information – drip-feed them.

47_ When leading routes with novice climbers, leave the camming devices in your sack if you want to keep them.

48_ Generally people can only take in five new pieces of information at once. If they're stressed this number decreases, so you may find that they can only remember one thing.

49_ Just because someone puts in a good performance, doesn't mean they will perform to the same standard if you change the environment.

50_ When climbing in series or parallel, use different coloured ropes of the same thickness.

51_ Keep records of your ropes and equipment.

52_ Try to belay where you can see your seconds, even if that means that you don't belay where the guidebook suggests.

53_ When working on multi-pitch climbs, single-point belays (if you can achieve them) will make your life so much simpler.

54_ Single-point belays don't necessarily teach your clients anything.

55_ Teach your clients to back-coil the ropes at each stance, so that the leader's end of the rope is at the top of the pile. This will minimise tangles and twists.

56_ Sort out the rack while your clients back-coil the ropes.

57_ On a single-pitch crag, do you need to untie after each route?

58_ Gear up away from the base of the crag so that you are less likely to be hit by anything falling from above.

59_ Think about why and where you are working. Would a climbing wall be somewhere better to run the 'team building' climbing session than the local crag?

60_ Always address your group by their names, particularly

when you need them to do something important.

61_ If you can't remember their names, use

sticky labels on their helmets.

62_ If you can work out how your clients learn, you can

work out the best methods for teaching them.

63_ If you take time to explain to someone why they
are doing something, you will often see much
better results when it's their turn to give it a go.

64_ There is a big difference between a rule and a guideline.

65_ Rules are for the guidance of wise men and
the obedience of fools – Douglas Bader.

66   Use the walk-in to listen to your group and observe how they are moving – are they stable on their feet or do they stumble with every step?

67   Just because you learn a new skill in a particular manner, doesn't mean that anyone else will.

68_ If you feel that your patience is wearing thin, then

stop, take a breath and think about what you are trying

to achieve. Then try again, or change your tack.

69_ There is no such thing as thick client, only a bad instructor.

70_ If you run sessions off the cuff, at some

point you will be caught out!

71_ Talk less, observe more.

72_ Think before you give feedback.

73_ Are there ways that you can increase

participation within your group?

74_   When giving feedback, less is often more.

75_   Keep instructions to the minimum safely required
       to allow maximum time for the activity.

76_   Use language that is appropriate for the group. There is
       no point in using language that they don't understand.

77. Teach the group technical climbing

language when they need it.

78. Move from simple to complex techniques over time.

79. Practice skills randomly and in the widest

range of environments possible.

80_ When giving specific feedback on a technique,

offer ideas on how to improve it.

81_ You don't always have to speak to give feedback.

82_ Asking questions as part of feedback will help you to

discover how well the group really understand the task.

83_ Keep instructions clear and simple.

84_ Some people like being treated like mushrooms,

the majority do not – don't keep them in

the dark about what you are doing!

85_ Grades aren't the be-all and end-all of climbing.

86_ Appropriately used, a guidebook with the grades removed is a good tool to help with the mental issues associated with breaking through of personal grade boundaries.

87_ If you can't see your group, you don't know what they are doing.

88_ If you don't know what your group is doing,

how can you say you are in control?

89_ When setting up a top rope, first tie the rope around

a boulder and throw the end of the rope down the

crag. That way, other crag users know which route you

are planning to use and can discuss it with you.

90_ Remember that you have as much right as anyone

else to use a climb or section of crag.

91_ You don't have the right to hog a particular

climb or section of crag for long periods.

92_ It's good manners to discuss the use of

particular routes or crags with other users.

93. Drink plenty before and during the day to avoid headaches.

94. You can use pieces of hose pipe, split

lengthways, as rope protectors.

95. A group with time on their hands and nothing to do will

find something to do. It won't always be sensible!

96_ To engage a group while you are rigging an abseil

place a rope down a gentle slope or on flat ground

and allow them to work out how to put the

abseil device on the rope and how it works.

97_ When teaching belaying using a Gri-Gri, remember that the device is not foolproof. You need to teach correct belaying technique, as you would with any other type of belay device.

98. You are more likely to inspire a group to do something by being willing to do it yourself, particularly something that they don't like such as picking up litter.

99. Be familiar with a whole range of belay devices, as you never know what your clients will turn up with.

100. If you feel the need to place more than three anchors

when building a bottom rope or top rope system,

you may not be using the most sensible venue.

101. The more complex the belay system, the

longer it will take for you to make.

102_ Give the group a guidebook and get them
to work out where they are climbing.

103_ Give the group a guidebook and allow them to
select the routes that they wish to climb.

104_ A warm-up doesn't involve stretching at all.

105_ A warm-up exercises the heart and
lungs, and lubricates the joints.

106_ A good warm-up will allow you to observe your group
and to judge what their movement skills are like.

107_ You can use the warm-up to introduce skills that
you will use during the rest of the session.

108_ Paying a climbing coach will improve your climbing.

109_ Match your belay plates to the diameter
of the rope that you are using.

110_ One of the hardest decisions that you can make is
deciding when a client can belay on their own.

111_ If you can find a venue with several routes that you
can rig using one set of anchors, just by retying a
few knots, you will save yourself a lot of time.

112_ Having clients spot each other is a simple way
of increasing participation, without increasing
the number of people climbing.

113_   Build in time to allow yourself to think during your sessions.

114_   Supervise only as many clients as you feel happy with.

115_   With some clients, you may need to have a higher

staff ratio even as many as two staff to each client.

116_ Not every group will behave the same.

117_ Challenge poor behaviour and language.

118_ Remember the hierarchy of gear placement;
natural, passive and then non-passive.

119_ Camming devices are not usually appropriate for bottom rope systems as repeated loading and unloading may cause the cam to walk, which you will not be able to monitor from the belay stance.

120_ The most important part of the day is the ten minutes in the café, discussing and agreeing a plan for the day.

121. The second most important part of the day is the review of the session at the end of the day, when you can highlight what you have all achieved.

122. Use belay bags or ground anchors even with groups that don't need them, as it stops them wandering around.

123_ Make sure that helmets fit correctly. Have a way

of checking this before getting to the venue.

124_ A spare woolly hat worn underneath a helmet may help

to get a better, more comfortable fit with small heads.

125_ The belly button marks the location of the waist, not the hips!

126_ A spotter doesn't catch; they redirect a fall, while protecting the climber's head, neck and back.

127_ Protect the environment that you are working in. No one else will.

128_ Once a groove has been made in the rock (by ropes rubbing over the edge) it will be there forever.

129. You can cut through a tensioned, full weight, single rope with a piece of prussic cord. Imagine what a sharp edge can do.

130. Try to minimise the number of links in your belay system.

131. The more links in the system, the greater the potential for errors.

132. A gritstone or granite crag can destroy a new climbing rope
in a matter of minutes if the system that you are using
allows the moving rope to come into contact with the rock.

133. A rope may last five years, but you could
damage it permanently on its first outing.

134_ A harness is designed to trap the hips between the waist belt and the leg loops.

135_ A full-body harness gives people a full-body hug and generally makes them feel safer.

136_ Use a full-body harness with people that don't have hips that stick out – children and men with beer bellies.

137_ If you haven't got a full-body harness, you can use a sit harness combined with a chest harness.

138_ You can improvise a chest harness using a sling, but it needs to tied off in such a way that it can't tighten on the climbers chest.

139_ Use a manmade object for your group abseil session. It cuts down on crag erosion.

140_ If you are working with the same clients for some time, aim to make them independent so they no longer need you.

141_ If you are working with clients for a short session, aim to make them leave thinking that climbing is brilliant fun.

142_ Every instructor needs to know how people learn.

143_ Allow clients to make a decision and commit

to it before you say or do anything.

144_ If you allow your client to check everything with you

every time, what will they do when you're not there?

145_ With a poorly behaved group, don't threaten to do something that you can't possibly do or are unwilling to carry out.

146_ If you are going to carry a small penknife, don't have it on the back of your harness but in an easily accessible pocket.

147_ Plasters (as a minimum) in a ziplock bag may be useful on multi-pitch routes.

148_ In winter, carry your prussic cords in an easily accessible pocket. That way they will not be frozen, or covered by your rucksack.

149_ Kneel down when helping a client to adjust their harness; you will be in a less threatening position.

150_ When adjusting a client's harness, position yourself to one side, so that everyone can see what you are doing.

151_ When it comes to safeguarding young people, don't put yourself in a position where an allegation can be made against you.

152_ It takes years to build a good reputation
but seconds to destroy one.

153_ When adjusting harnesses or helmets, always
ask permission to touch someone and make
sure you tell them what you are doing.

154_   Join the appropriate professional association – the
       Mountain Leader Training Association (MLTA) or
       Association of Mountaineering Instructors (AMI).

155_   You need to have a valid first aid certificate in order
       for your MLT awards to be considered valid.

156_ Keep your logbook up to date; it's an important document that can demonstrate your range and breadth of experience. If it's empty it won't show anyone anything.

157_ There is no place for egos in teaching. Leave your's at home.

158. You can demonstrate how and why to extend runners and the effect that a fall has on a leader's protection using your gear, a rope and a few tent pegs on a flat piece of ground.

159. Belayers should be as close to the foot of the wall as possible. It makes it much safer for the lead climber.

160_ If someone is too scared they won't be in a position to learn to the best of their ability.

161_ Having a few bolt hangers and spare bolts are useful when teaching certain skills on artificial walls, but can only be used in non-load bearing situations.

162_ When a demonstration is required, get one group that can already do it to demonstrate. Watching their peers is more likely to encourage the others into thinking they can succeed.

163_ If an instructor does a demonstration, the group may be left thinking 'of course they can do it, they're the expert!' and become de-motivated.

164_ Take individuals back to basics when teaching them about balance and its role within climbing.

165_ Self-arrest is a complex skill to learn and practice. Walking is something we practice every time we go out. Help your winter groups to learn to walk better rather than just focusing on what to do if they slip.

166_ Teach people to keep their axe in their uphill hand so that they can grab the shaft near the snow and check a slip. This is much better than picking up speed and having to self-arrest.

167_ When teaching self-arrest, simplify the process by teaching body movements without an axe.

168_ You don't know for certain that they are carrying

it unless you have seen it go in their rucksack.

169_ Put helmets on early and take them

off late, especially in winter.

170_ Running a group abseil is technically the most difficult

situation to rig well and the most difficult to manage safely.

171_ Working in busy venues isn't just a summer crag issue. Discuss your concerns with other winter climbers if their chosen rope system is likely to put you and your students at risk.

172_ Avoid working on or beneath thawing, busy crags.

173_ Always think twice before following someone up
an ice route. Will your team be showered with ice?
Can you site clients' belays out of the fall line?

174_ If you always short-rope clients who want to
learn to winter climb to and from the routes, how
will they cope when you aren't there?

175_ Thread crampon straps under a lace on the toe of the boot. If it does come off, it won't fall down the crag.

176_ If they need to learn to do it in winter, get them to practice it in winter gloves. Also try it one-handed.

177_ One day spent learning dry tooling can make a grade of difference to the students' technique on winter climbs.

178_ Don't follow the guidebook slavishly, especially in winter. Making up a route from interesting features may give your students a quieter day or a better learning experience. You might get a new route out of it as well!

179_ When teaching winter climbing, remember to clip your students' axes to the belay.

180_ In winter be honest about your ethics. Make

sure your clients understand when a route is

in condition and why this is important.

181_ If you are cold, wet and uncomfortable they probably are too!

182_ Silk liners make it much easier to change a wet pair of gloves.

183_   Learn to lead from anywhere in the group, not just the front.

184_   Tiny lightweight krabs are great in summer

but hard to grip with winter gloves.

185_   Watch as many other people at work as possible.

Some of the tools they use won't work for you or

suit your style, but many will or can be adapted.

186_ When you've stopped learning it's time to quit teaching.

187_ Only tell your clients what they need to know just now, not what you would like them to know.

188_ When teaching the leader don't forget the belayer.

189_ Don't give them an answer if you can get them
to answer the question themselves.

190_ When giving feedback choose a moment when
they will be receptive – not at the crux!

191_ Give the climber time to process what has just
happened to them before you give them feedback.

192_ Falling off is what climbers do – teach it.

193_ Questions can draw out the deeper learning
and understanding in an individual. It's up to
you to work out the right questions to ask.

194_ Don't overuse questioning; it can really annoy people.

195_ Used well, questioning is a powerful tool. Used badly it can be destructive. Like any other skill you need to learn how to use it correctly.

196_ If your assessor asks you why you have done something, don't assume that you are wrong. They just want to understand your decision.

197_ Don't second-guess your assessor; you'll be trying to work out what they want, instead of concentrating on what you should be doing.

198_ If you're not sure of something, it's up to you to ask someone who knows the answer! Ignorance is not an excuse.

199_ If you are standing in front of your belay plate, you cannot effectively lock it off.

200_ If you need to stand in front of your belay device, use an Italian hitch.

201_ Make sure that your belay plate is correctly orientated so that you can easily lock it off.

202_ It is your problem if the group or
individual doesn't understand.

203_ Encourage climbers to spot places to rest on a route
before they start climbing. Break the route down
into little chunks, using these resting places.

204_ Finding somewhere comfortable to rest often means that a novice lead climber is able to place protection that they are happier to believe will stay in place.

205_ Your judgement is your most important quality as a climbing instructor.

206_ Good judgement comes from experience. Experience comes from bad judgement! – Steve Long, *On the Edge* (1986).

207_ When rock climbing, soloing in clear sight of clients does not set a good example and isn't good practice.

208_ Boasting to and showing off in front of your clients just makes you look foolish.

209_ You don't have to climb better than your students, you just need to be safe.

210_ A climbing instructor assessment is a bit like your driving test; you often have the minimum amount of experience and still have a lot of learning to do!

211_ As an instructor you need to be able to
belay both left and right handed.

212_ When working at the top of the crag, position yourself and
rig your system in such a way that you are comfortable
and so your group don't have to climb over the ropes.

213_ Some clients will copy and others will mirror, your movements. It's up to you to work out where you need to stand in order to be in the best position so that all of the group can learn.

214_ A well-planned warm-up is a good place to work out how your clients learn. You can also use it to find out who copies and who mirrors your movements.

215 Use video to analyse and critique your technique.

216 Try giving just verbal instructions and
see who can follow them.

217 Try giving just visual instructions and
see who can follow them.

218_ Some people are 'doers' – after giving instructions allow them to go and try while you give more direct input to those that want it.

219_ Sometimes all it takes is a slight bit of pressure from a spotter to help the climber to do the move. But how does this help them?

220_ Use the rope to build belays, leaving

your slings to extend runners.

221_ Suggest rock shoes that are a size bigger if

you are going to be in them all day.

222_ Always wear a helmet.

223_ A link of karabiners is a good way to shockload and
      remove jammed gear if your nut key can't do the job.

224_ Long extenders can be shortened, short
      extenders can't be lengthened.

225_ When teaching leading, simulate it first
      so it's not such a big thing.

226_ Dirty shoes make routes a grade harder – clean them.

227_ To clean dirty shoes carry a beer towel.

228_ When teaching wear the same shoes as your
clients. Wearing approach shoes when they are
in rock boots may belittle their achievements.

229_ On multi-pitch routes time is lost on belays.

Save the information for when you leave

the stance and keep things moving.

230_ Why do we use chalk?

231_ Scrambling is not an activity for wet

days. Choose an easy route.

232_ Being faster at your belay changeover is
better than having to climb fast.

233_ After a cold winter or heavy storm, expect routes to
have loose holds and test before pulling on them.

234_ Fill your pockets with food before starting a multi-pitch route.

235_ Carry a head torch on long routes.

236_ Prussic loops make good bits of tat but use them sparingly.

237_ When retreating use the gear you need, not less. You can buy new gear but not a new spine or skull.

238_ On multi-pitch routes, carry a double set of wires shared across three or four karabiners in case you drop some.

239_ Carry cams and hexes on their own karabiners or in small sets, not as one big bunch.

240_ It is rare to use RPs and micro nuts on routes below VS.

241_ Slings don't stretch as much as ropes do.

242_ On multi-pitch routes start your day with lots

of layers on – it's easy to remove layers to

cool off, but being cold all day is grim.

243_ Carry a little spare food for when your clients forget their's.

244_ Guidebooks get trashed, so if you use one area a lot consider photocopying the relevant pages only – you are allowed to do this for your personal use.

245_ Keep slings over your head and shoulder on a karabiner; that way you can release a sling with either hand on hard pitches.

246_ Backing off routes happens – prepare for it.

247_ At the end of each day reorganise your rack

to help avoid losing equipment.

248_ Hair and fingers can get trapped if you don't take precautions.

249_ If you make a mistake or have a near miss,

report it to your employer – they may discover

trends and revise the risk assessment.

250_ You are responsible for your own ongoing

dynamic risk assessment.

251_ When teaching clients on ledges, always check

screwgates as it's easy to leave them undone.

252_ Don't keep screwgates on your harness

screwed up, leave them undone.

253_ Some days it's appropriate to finish early and rest.

254_ Climbing is like eating an elephant –

you have to do it in bite-size chunks.

255_ Harnesses and helmets need re-checking

after toilet breaks or lunch.

256_ When teaching multi-pitch climbing, think CLAP (Communication, Line of sight, Avoidance is better than cure, Position of most usefulness).

257_ If you expect your group to wear a helmet, do you wear one too?

258_ Anchors, belayer, climber (ABC) in line.

259_ When you are climbing for yourself it is fine to wear those old ripped and tatty clothes, but does it send the right message when you are working with groups?

260_ Use insulation tape so you can recognise your own kit.

261_ Don't blindly trust in situ gear; you can't see what is going on beneath the surface!

262_ Your jacket is like your office or your desk – use a

filing system that works for you and stick to it.

263_ Buy a helmet that is so comfortable

that you forget you have it on.

264_ It is easier to carry a tiny emergency head torch than to

change a set of batteries at night or in a blizzard (or both).

265_ Make sure students know to bring a thin hat
if they are going to be wearing a helmet.

266_ Few plans survive their first trial. Stay flexible and
don't be afraid to change the plan in response
to weather, conditions other parties.

267_ Gaining an award means it is time to start learning to use it.

268_ 'Bank time' by being efficient at the beginning of the day in case you need it at the end.

269_ Be bothered – do the little jobs like recoiling the rope, adjusting zips, laces and straps right the first time to save yourself time, energy and problems later. Teach your clients to be bothered too.

270_ Keep your abalakov threader or nut key on a
retracting ski pass holder to stop you dropping it.

271_ Watch and learn from other instructors. You will find
that you like some things that they do, but not others.

272_ When working with clients you need to know what their
current level of ability is – don't take their word for it.

273. Teach your clients how to observe. Then, with help, they can observe and coach each other.

274. When observing, if you spot something wait to see if it appears again before you address it – make sure that it is not a one-off.

275_ Make the last five words of your verbal
instruction the important ones.

276_ You instruct and coach people first, climbing second.
Make sure that you address the person's needs first.

277_ A good indication that your clients need a break
is when their performance drops suddenly.

278_ Make sure your group rest before trying a strenuous problem again – they will be more likely to succeed.

279_ People value you for the quality of your feedback, not the amount.

280_ More visual feedback, more kinaesthetic feedback and much less audio feedback will improve your coaching performance.

281_ If climbing with two clients, get one of them to build the belays and bring up the third climber.

282_ Practise your ascending method before teaching leading on a fixed line.

283_ Re-belay your fixed line to reduce stretch on longer pitches or crags.

284_ Just because you've done it that way for the last twenty

years doesn't mean that there isn't a better way.

285_ If a challenging member of the group is doing

something daft, just point out what and why and then

turn away. Confrontation is counter-productive.

286_ Watch the belayer more than the climber, or at

least have a system to back them up.

287_ Use rules for novices. Use principles for intermediates.

288_ Principles require understanding.

Understanding requires experience.

289_ There are always effective and creative
ways of solving a problem.

290_ Clients don't always know their own abilities
or experience – assess them yourself.

291_ While assessing keep your eyes and
ears open and your mouth shut.

292_   Effective coaching requires excellent knowledge
       of a sport, not excellent ability.

293_   Don't let climbs defeat you. Find a way up, even by
       pulling on gear. This will minimise mental barriers and
       keep you positive. Back off only if it's dangerous.

294_   Focus, relax and breathe – all the time.

295_ For quick clips put the quickdraw onto the neck of your T shirt. You don't have to look down when you clip and it's very fast.

296_ Get your clients to select gear for cracks by sight and see if it fits. Encourage them to practise this regularly so that they get first-time selections as much as possible.

297_ On steep ice, try climbing as you would do on a climbing wall – silently. That means hooking as much as possible with straight arms, kicking light first-time placements every time and moving fluidly in balance. Imagine you are rock climbing.

298_ An expert is someone who has made and survived more mistakes than most. Get out and make your own.

299_ Judgement requires experience. The best experience requires mistakes.

300_ Expert coaching requires; defined outcomes – assess what your clients really want and what they are prepared to do to get it.

301_ Expert coaching requires; sensory acuity –

being able to observe or detect fine details.

302_ Expert coaching requires; behavioural flexibility –

using different strategies and actions to achieve results.

303_ Expert coaching requires; rapport – the ability to

create trust and understanding with your clients.

304_ Coach the whole person – don't concentrate only on skill. There's also knowledge, attitude, fitness and more.

305_ It's very hard to talk your way out of self-limiting beliefs; it is much better to change your behaviour. Make your client do something small that they thought they couldn't do and go on from there.

306_ There's no such thing as failure – only feedback.

307_ Expert athletes are very good at visualising
– encourage this in your clients.

308_ When teaching leading, make sure that you are
carrying a small rack so that you can place additional
protection for your client if they need it.

309_ Try to rig your fixed line to one side of the route that your client is trying to lead so that you don't get in the way.

310_ Teach good habits from the start.

311_ Climbing is a team sport – we rely on others to make it safer.

312_ Always get the group to check each
      other's helmets and harnesses.

313_ Set a good example – get one of your clients
      to check your helmet and harness.

314_ When teaching leading, give them time to practice
      placing protection along the bottom of the crag.

315_ Don't slip into negative teaching – "Don't do it like this." Quite often people will remember only what you showed them and not the correct way.

316_ If you are using peer belaying with a second person backing-up the rope, the rope between the belayer and back-up should create a 'smiley face'.

317_ When teaching leading, the most important thing is get the progression right for the client: Top-roping. Lead on pre-placed protection. Lead on pre-placed protection at critical points and placing their own protection in between. Finally, placing all their own protection with you alongside.

318_ The best training for climbing is climbing.

319_ Use 11mm rope with novice groups – it lasts longer and is more forgiving in a peer belaying situation. There are usually plenty of people to carry gear to the crag so the slight increase in weight won't be a problem.

320_ Choose a place to abseil with care to avoid destroying classic climbs.

321_ Analyse your day afterwards and try to think of any ways you could improve it.

322_ An understanding of how we learn climbing moves is important. Our brains learn moves and sequences of moves by repetition, so that eventually we make many moves without really thinking about it.

323_ You should know your venue so that you already have a session plan in your mind and can set up the first climbs quickly; try to get this done within fifteen minutes.

324_ Choose your group equipment carefully so that it will do the job. This will depend on the main type of group and the venues to be used.

325_ Always use a stopper knot when tying in with a re-threaded figure-of-eight. While it is unlikely to come undone if a long tail is left, it can still be mis-tied. A stopper knot means that the knot is still relatively safe.

326_ If you can tie a stopper knot, you have definitely left a long enough tail.

327_ Teach clients to store their belay plate on the back of their harness when not in use. That way it is difficult to accidentally belay on a gear loop!

328_ Time in winter is precious. If one member of a group has to stop, the others should use the time to avoid having to stop later. Eat something, take a pee, adjust your layering …

329_ An Italian hitch is most efficient when the live and dead ropes are parallel. Rig your system so this can happen.

330_ Avalanche awareness isn't just about digging snowpits. It's about dozens of tiny observations made throughout the day. Bring these to a conscious level and share the process with your clients.

331_ Teach people how to avoid faffing. Get them to do a dry run in their head of what they need to do before they stop to do it.

332_ You wouldn't like waiting for clients so don't make them wait for you.

333_ In winter, if the car park is full you are possibly setting off too late.

334_ If you are going to stop to do something, give the rest of the group five minutes warning so that they can plan how to make best use of the time.

335_ Stop at the bottom of the steep walking section and encourage people to remove layers before they start sweating.

336_ Most of the things that make you a fast, slick climber are not easily learnt. Bring them to a conscious level and share them with your clients.

337_ Enjoy yourself – because the group will know if you're not.

Notes

Notes